Ceolta Seisiúin na hÉireann

Irish Session Tunes

The Blue Book

Irish Session Tunes – in Sets
Selected by Bríd Cranitch

OSSIAN

Published by
Ossian Publications

Exclusive Distributors:
Hal Leonard
7777 West Bluemound Road, Milwaukee, WI 53213
Email: info@halleonard.com
Hal Leonard Europe Limited
42 Wigmore Street Maryleborne, London, WIU 2 RN
Email: info@halleonardeurope.com
Hal Leonard Australia Pty. Ltd.
4 Lentara Court Cheltenham, Victoria, 9132 Australia
Email: info@halleonard.com.au

Order No. OMB85
ISBN 1-900428-82-2
This book © Copyright 2003 Novello & Company Limited

Music design by Andrew Shiels
Portraits by Brian Denington

Design by John Loesberg

Printed in EU.

www.halleonard.com

Other titles in this range of session tunes books are:

Irish Session Tunes, The Orange Book
by Bríd Cranitch, OMB 153   ISBN 1 900428 17 2
CD edition OMB84 ISBN 1-900428-77-6
Irish Session Tunes, The Green Book
by Geraldine Cotter, OMB 141 ISBN 1 900428 56 3
Irish Session Tunes, The Red Book
by Matt Cranitch, OMB 142   ISBN 1 900428 61 X

Foreword

A number of years ago, as an apprentice fiddle player, I was struck by the way certain tunes seemed to fit very nicely with other tunes and that unless you knew how to get from one tune to the next (ie. with a suitable linking note sequence), you simply 'crashed'!

Another thing I noticed was that, as learners, we usually learn tunes one at the time and when we feel 'ready', we go off to play in a session. What often happens then is that we find it hard to 'fit in' the tunes we've learnt because, in a session, tunes are played in sets of 2 to 3 tunes per set (minimum !). In other words, the tunes that fit nicely together are played together !

The tunes that make up each set vary from region to region and are also dependent on the instruments being played in the session, as there are 'fiddle' tunes and 'box' tunes, for example. What's more, there are tunes that go in and out of fashion ! (I recall the reel 'The Clumsy Lover' being played very frequently a number of years back, but it has obviously gone out of fashion because I have not heard it for ages !) Then there are, of course, the 'classics' which are heard in sessions no matter where you are and what instruments are being played, for example 'Cooley's' and 'The Wise Maid'.

The best approach to learning the tunes is to learn (i) the first tune, (ii) then the first and second tune, (paying special attention to the ending of the first tune and the start of the second tune) and finally (iii) the entire set (again being careful going from one tune to the next).

Each set is numbered 1, 2, 3, 4 etc and the tunes are numbered .1, .2, .3, .4, etc. Therefore a full set, of say 3 tunes, is numbered 1.1, 1.2, 1.3, for example.

This collection of session-tunes-sets is by no means definitive in nature. But rather, is based on the many sessions I have listened to and played in, making mental notes and scribbling down tunes on scraps of paper !

I am very grateful to the many fine musicians I have heard at sessions and who keep the music alive and well. I am especially indebted to musicians like Connie O' Connell, Dennis Mc Mahon, Matt Cranitch, Aidan Coffey, Jackie Daly and Seanie O' Driscoll who assisted me with many of the tune names. However, some tunes still remain nameless !

And to the learners - I hope this collection helps to bridge the gap between the learning and the session playing !

As regards the CD, each part of the tune is played twice but the tune itself is only played once. The first time round is played as closely as possible to the written music, while the second time round may vary, as often happens in traditional playing. In the case of single reels – the entire tune is played twice.

The marathon recording of all the tunes would not have been possible without the great and infectious playing of Sheila Garry and indeed would not have been such fun to make without her great sense of fun and enthusiasm ! Thanks Sheila !

Bríd Cranitch

Index

1.1 Wandering Minstrel (Jig)

1.2 Fasten the Leg In Her (Jig)

2.1 Charlie Harris' Reel (Reel)

2.2 Mick O' Connor's (Reel)

3.1 Doughie McFay's (Reel)

3.2 Andy Dickson's (Reel)

4.1 Wheels of the World (Jig)

4.2 Pat McGillarney's (Jig)

5.1 Trip to Durrow (Reel)

5.2 The Ships are Sailing (Reel)

6.1 Tarbolton (Reel)

6.2 Longford Collector (Reel)

6.3 Sailor's Bonnet (Reel)

7.1 Rose in the Heather (Jig)

7.2 Rambler (Jig)

8.1 Galtee Ranger (Reel)

8.2 The Gleanntán (Reel)

8.3 O'Callaghan's (Reel)

9.1 Hunter's Purse (Reel)

9.2 Congress (Reel)

9.3 O'Rourke's (Reel)

10.1 Luck Penny (Jig)

10.2 Tobin's Favourite (Jig)

11.1 Haste to the Wedding (Jig)

11.2 Saddle the Pony (Jig)

11.3 Father O'Flynn's (Jig)

12.1 Blacksmith (Reel)

12.2 Cup of Tea (Reel)

13.1 Lad O'Beirne's (Reel)

13.2 Shetland (Reel)

14.1 Tatter Jack Walsh (Jig)

14.2 Garret Barry (Jig)

15.1 Volunteer (Reel)

15.2 Old Pigeon on the Gate (Reel)

16.1 Flax in Bloom (Reel)

16.2 Dairy Maid (Reel)

17.1 Scholar (Reel)

17.2 Teetotaller (Reel)

17.3 St. Anne's (Reel)

18.1 Whelan's (Jig)

18.2 Clare Jig

18.3 Humours of Glendart (Jig)

19.1 Humours of Ballydaly (Slide)

19.2 Dan O'Keeffe's (Slide)

19.3 Brosna Slide No.1

19.4 Brosna Slide No.2

20.1 Connie O'Connell's (Jig)

20.2 Frost is all Over (Jig)

21.1 Lark on the Strand (Jig)

21.2 Knights of St. Patrick (Jig)

22.1 Mulhaire's (Reel)

22.2 Roger Sherlock's (Reel)

23.1 Rolling in the Rye Grass (Reel)

23.2 Duke of Leinster (Reel)

23.3 Wind That Shakes the Barley (Reel)

24.1 Munster Buttermilk (Jig)

24.2 Humours of Lisheen (Jig)

25.1 Padraig O'Keeffe's (Slide)

25.2 Dark Girl in Blue (Slide)

25.3 Kaiser (Slide)

26.1 Orphan (Jig)

26.2 Clancy's (Jig)

26.3 Dan Collin's Father's (Jig)

27.1 Broken Pledge (Reel)

27.2 Crib of Perches (Reel)

27.3 Geoghegan's (Reel)

28.1 Jacket of Batteries (Reel)

28.2 Templehouse (Reel)

28.3 Kiss Me Kate (Reel)

29.1 Gallagher's Frolics (Jig)

29.2 Bímis ag Ól (Jig)

29.3 Have A Drink With Me (Jig)

30.1 Cordal Jig (Jig)

30.2 A d'tiocfaidh tú abhaile liom? (Jig)

30.3 Humours of Ballinafad (Jig)

31.1 Thadelo's (Barndance)

31.2 No Name (Barndance)

32.1 No Name (Polka)

32.2 Lackagh Cross (Polka)

32.3 No Name (Polka)

33.1 Tuar Mór No.1 (Polka)

33.2 Tuar Mór No.2 (Polka)

33.3 Hayden's Fancy (Polka)

34.1 Drowsey Maggie (Reel)

34.2 Cooley's (Reel)

34.3 Wise Maid (Reel)

35.1 Free and Easy (Reel)

35.2 Drunken Landlady (Reel)

35.3 Mulvihill's (Reel)

36.1 Silver Spear (Reel)

36.2 Miss McCloud's (Reel)

37.1 Miss Monaghan's (Reel)

37.2 Miss Johnson's (Reel)

38.1 Miss Langford's (Reel)

38.2 Red-Haired Lass (Reel)

39.1 Monsignor's Blessing (Reel)

39.2 Limerick Lasses (Reel)

40.1 Fermoy Lassies (Reel)

40.2 Hand Me Down the Tackle (Reel)

Printed in the EU.